*SOME OF THESE RECIPES CALL FOR EXACT AMOUNTS WHILE OTHERS ARE GREAT IDEAS FOR FLAVOR COMBINATIONS. WHEN MIXING A DRINK, FEEL FREE TO ADJUST ACCORDING TO YOUR PERSONAL TASTE. AND, OF COURSE, ABIDE BY YOUR LOCAL LAWS REGARDING SERVING AND CONSUMING ALCOHOL!

IN ORDER OF APPEARANCE...

TALL BLONDE by Ingvard the Terrible fr
007 MARTINI by Anthony Jandrokovic fi
BEE-STUNG LIPS by Logan Wagoner from Atlanta, GA (behance.net/loganwagoner)
TANGERINE DREAM by Salli Swindell from Hudson, OH (studiosss.com)
OLD FASHION by Jeffrey Baratta from San Francisco, CA (jeffbarattadesign.com)
SIDECAR by Rebecca Bradley from Baltimore, MD (rebeccabradley.wordpress.com)
VIVA EL MOJITO by Beril Aba from Turkey
GIN MARTINI by James Orndorf from Durango, CO (roughshelter.com)
BLOODY MARY by Tracy Mattocks from Nashville, TN (altpick.com/tracymattocks)
CAIPIRINHA by Pedro Menezes from São Paulo, Brazil (quadernocriacao.blogspot.com)
DARK & STORMY by Nate Padavick from North Bennington, VT (idrawmaps.com)
GIN FIZZ by Philippe Debongnie from Brussels, Belgium (philippedebongnie.be)
COCONUT LIME RUM by Salli Swindell from Hudson, OH (studiosss.com)
KIR ROYALE by Brooke Albrecht from Columbus, OH (brookealbrechtstudio.blogspot.com)
EMERALD ISLE MARTINI by Nate Padavick from North Bennington, VT (idrawmaps.com)
BLUSHING GEISHA by Lisa Graves from Medway, MA (lisagravesdesign.net)
3 HALLOWEEN COCKTAILS by Denise Plauche from Atlanta, GA
GRANDMA DIXIE'S HOLIDAY PUNCH by Sam Bennett from New York, NY (oheatdirt.blogspot.com)
MOSCOW HOLIDAY MULE by Pamela Nudel from Berkeley, CA (pamelanudel.com)
MISTELA DE CHIMAJÁ by James Orndorf from Durango, CO (roughshelter.com)
TOM & JERRY by Vidhya Nagarajan from St. Louis, MO (vidhyanagarajan.com)
CHAMPAGNE COCKTAIL by Nate Padavick from North Bennington, VT (idrawmaps.com)

007 MARTINI

3 MEASURES OF GORDONS GIN

1 MEASURE OF VODKA

1/2 MEASURE OF KINA LILLET

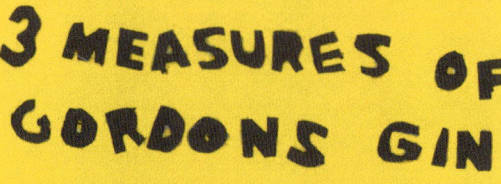

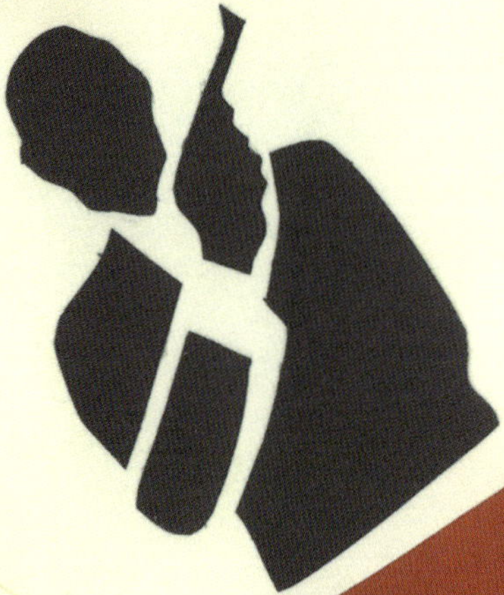

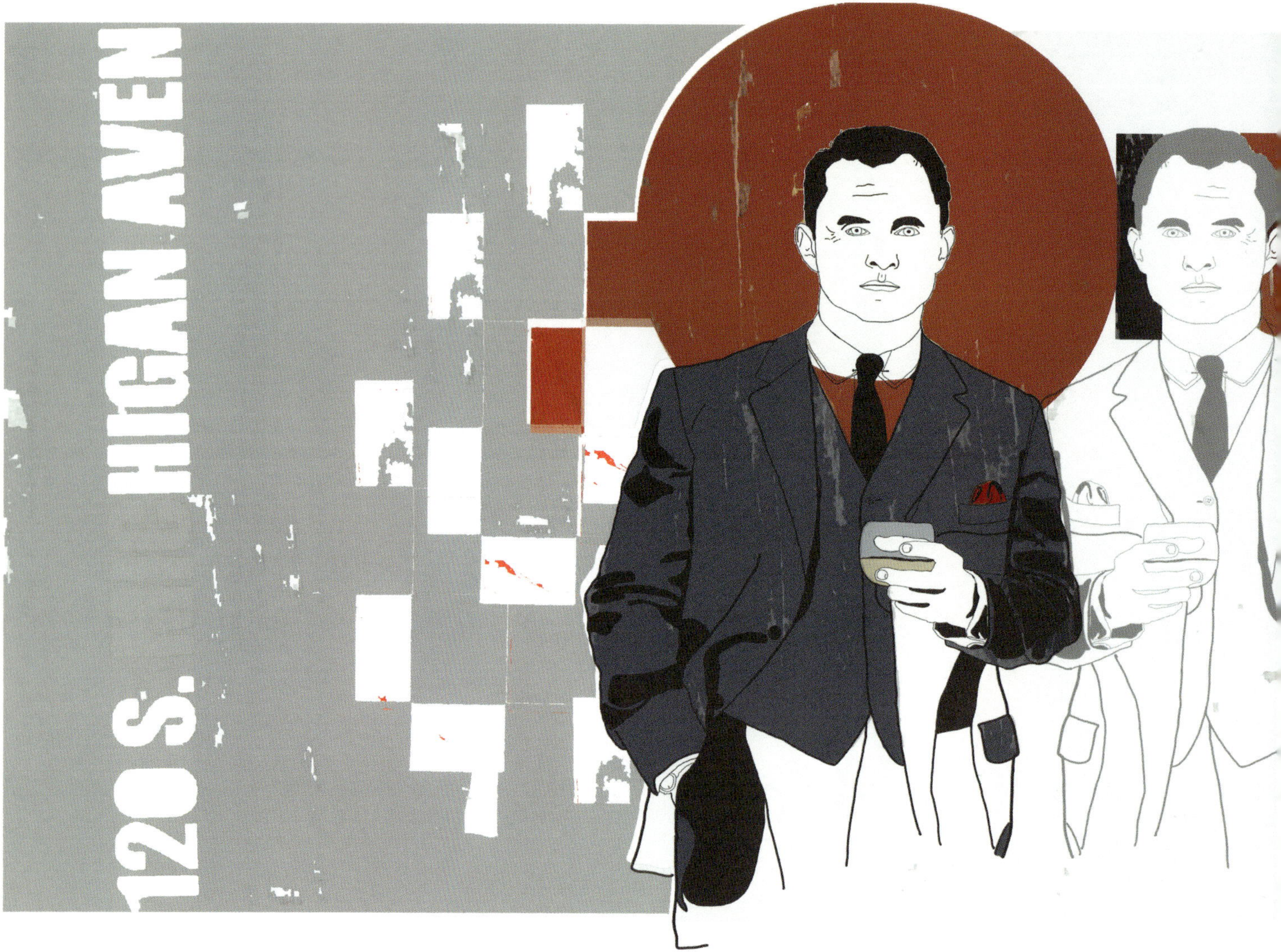
120 S. HIGAN AVEN

¡viva el mojito!

lime juice added to sugar.
mash mint leaves with a muddler.
rum is added. stir to dissolve sugar.
add sparkling soda.

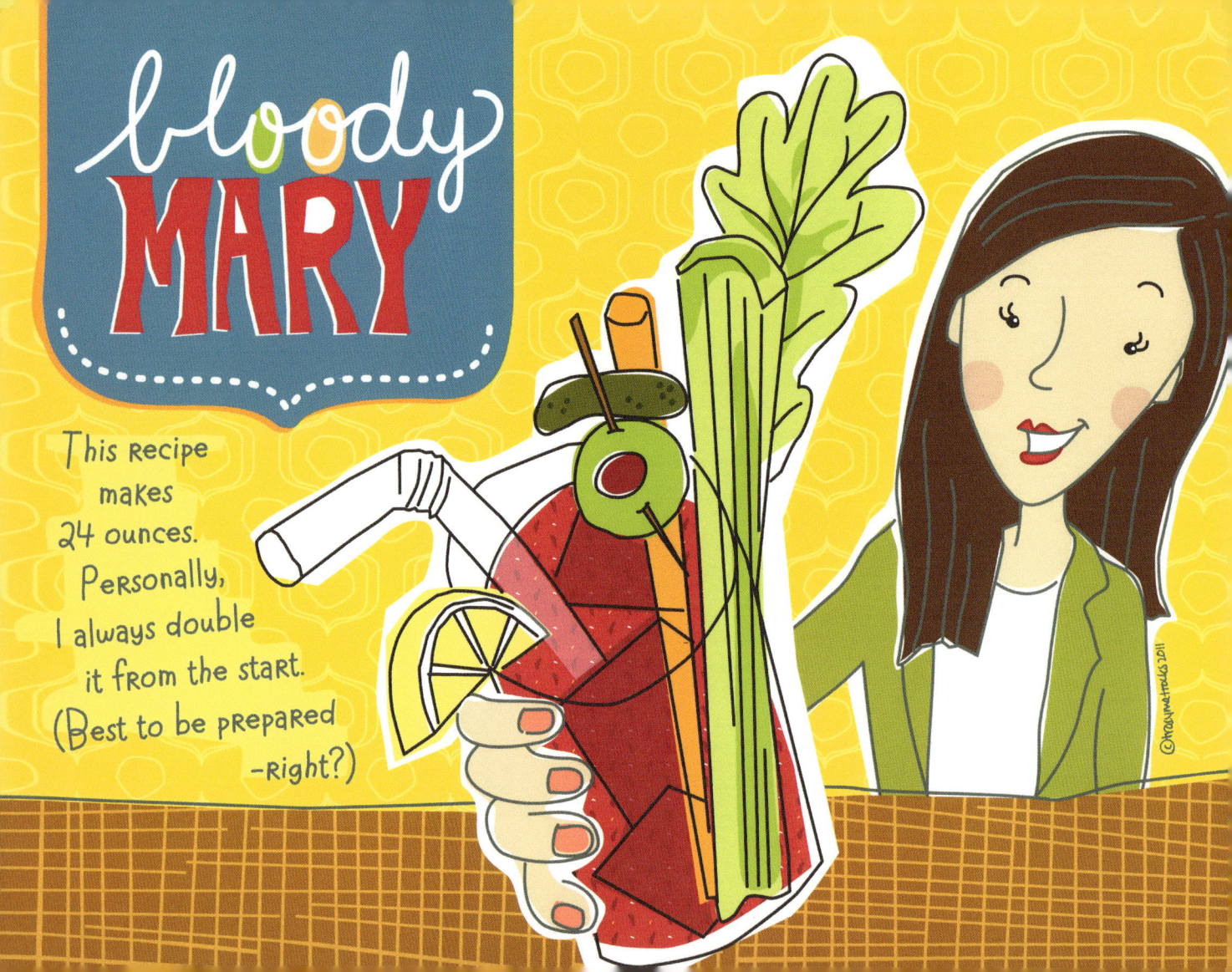

Here's what you'll need:

- 3 cups tomato juice
- 2 teaspoons prepared horseradish
- 1 teaspoon salt
- 1/2 teaspoon freshly ground pepper
- 1/2 teaspoon celery salt
- 1 1/2 teaspoons lemon juice
- 2 teaspoons Worcestershire sauce*
- 1/2 to 3/4 teaspoon hot sauce
- 1 clove garlic minced

*vegan Worcestershire sauce is available!

This recipe is by no means set in stone. Use this as a base and build from it!

Garnish Options:

- toothpick
- olives (green, black or kalamata)
- cornichons (mini pickles or any pickled veggie)
- pearl onion

other ideas: cucumbers, pepperoncini peppers, zucchini, grape tomatoes....be creative!

This is how you do it:

Put all ingredients into a container, seal container, then shake vigorously. Voila! Now you have your mix (which will stay good for a whole week)! In a glass of your choice add ice, celery stalk and carrot (if using), 1oz of vodka (or more, no judgment), then your mix and stir. Add garnish and enjoy your tasty concoction!

Mmmm!

Caipirinha is Brazil's national cocktail, made with cachaça, sugar and lime!

PREPARATION
Place lime and sugar into old fashioned glass and muddle (mash the two ingredients together using a muddler or a wooden spoon). Fill the glass with crushed ice and add the cachaça.

BLUSHING GEISHA

Mix together with crushed ice in a glass and garnish with fresh mint leaves

1 ounce Sake
2 fresh strawberries
½ ounce Strawberry Schnapps
1 teaspoon icing sugar
1 ounce Vodka

HALLOWE'EN COCKTAILS

Sour Witch
In the bottom of a mixing glass, muddle sour cherries in 1/2 oz. lime juice and 3/4 oz. almond syrup. Add 1 1/2 oz. absinthe with ice and shake very well. Strain into a chilled champagne flute. Top with sparkling wine or champagne. Garnish with freshly grated nutmeg.

Black Cat
Combine 1 oz. Kahlúa, 1 1/2 oz. vanilla vodka, and 1/4 oz. sambuca in a cocktail shaker filled with ice and stir. Strain into a chilled martini glass and garnish with 3 espresso beans.

Pumpkin Martini
Pour 1/2 oz. Sylk Cream Liqueur and 2 oz. vanilla vodka into a shaker filled with ice and shake well. Add 1/2 oz. pumpkin liqueur or pumpkin spice syrup and shake again. Strain into a chilled cocktail glass and top with a teaspoon of whipped cream. Garnish with a cinnamon stick.

MIX TOGETHER:

1 CAN FROZEN LIMEADE, THAWED
1 CAN FROZEN LEMONADE, THAWED
1 CAN FROZEN ORANGE JUICE, THAWED
1 LARGE BOTTLE OF APRICOT NECTAR
3 TWO-LITER BOTTLES GINGER ALE
VODKA, DIXIE SAYS AS MUCH AS YOU CAN HANDLE
ADD FRESH FRUIT FOR GARNISH, SUCH AS CRANBERRIES AND ORANGES
AND VOILÀ, IT'S PARTY TIME!

Moscow holiday mule

VODKA

SUGAR SYRUP

GINGER BEER

POUR OVER ICE:
2 oz. vodka
2 tsp. sugar syrup
1 cup ginger beer and
1 Tbs. lime juice.

GARNISH w/ lime, mint & a peppermint stick. Stir & ENJOY!

1 WHOLE DRIED ORANGE PEEL
4 STICKS CINNAMON
2 C. DRIED CHIMAJÁ ROOT
1 QUART WATER
1 POUND SUGAR

BOIL FOR 30 MIN.
STRAIN
MIX WITH 1 GALLON **WHISKEY**
BOTTLE
SET ASIDE FOR 2 WEEKS
OPEN ON CHRISTMAS

MISTELA DE CHIMAJÁ
A CHRISTMAS DRINK

FELIZ NAVIDAD

Tom and Jerry

Seperate an egg into 2 bowls. Add 1 oz. of Dark rum and 1 oz. of brandy to the yolk. Beat together.

In a different bowl beat the egg white till it peaks. Then, add 1 tsp. of sugar.

Continue to beat the sugar and egg white until stiff

Fold this into the mixture with the liquor. Pour into a coffee mug and top with coffee.

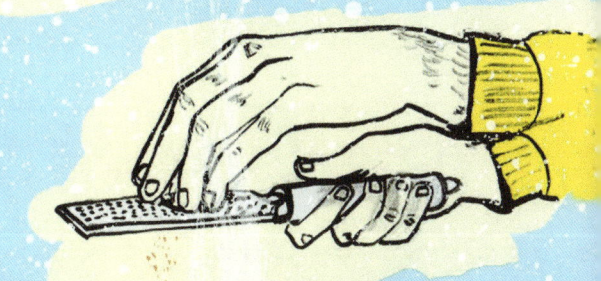

nutmeg for garnish

ENJOY!

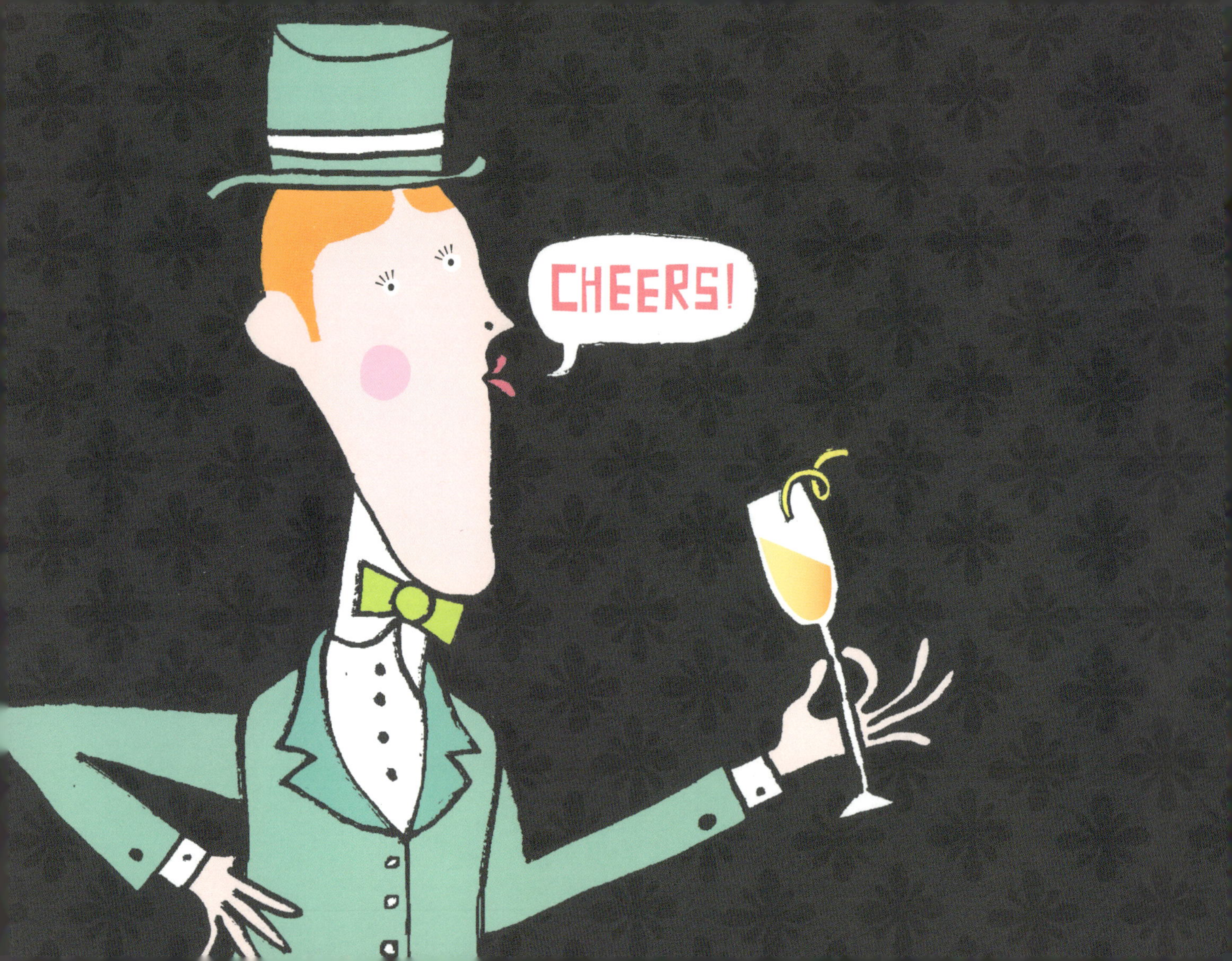
CHEERS!

Champagne Cocktail

BITTERS

SUGAR CUBE

A SPECIAL TOAST...

to the 16 wonderful artists whose recipes helped make this book possible. Your creativity, artistic talent and love of a good cocktail shine through on every page!

ANOTHER TOAST...

to the hundreds and hundreds of artists whose love of drawing and cooking can be enjoyed by all through the 3,000+ illustrated recipes on our website, *They Draw & Cook.*

AND LET'S (HICCUP) DRINK TO...

all the online fans and friends who generishly comment on and helf shpread the word about *They Cook & Draw*, I mean *They Draw & Cook.* Whatev. We luv u guyz. (hiccup)

BURP. AND, UM, HERE'S TO...

our pubrisher...huh? Oh yeah, we self-pubrished this boook. Drink it anyhow. Gulp, chug, (hiccup), oh boy.

ONE (BURP) LASHT TOASHT...

to Philippe Debongnie whose artwerk's on the covver. Phil, dude, yer (burp) awesohme man. C'mere giv ush a hug!

THANKSH EFFRYBUDDY! (HICCUP)

THEY DRAW & COOK™
Recipes Illustrated by Artists from Around the World

THE BEST ILLUSTRATED COCKTAIL RECIPES
CREATED BY ARTISTS FROM AROUND THE WORLD

Copyright © 2012 Studio SSS, LLC
All rights reserved, including the right of reproduction in whole or in part in any form.
Conceived, designed and produced by Studio SSS, LLC
theydrawandcook.com

STUDIO SSS, LLC
Nate Padavick & Salli Swindell
studiosss.com

The hand-lettered typeface used for the cover and interior text is called LINEDANCE and was created by Salli Swindell. This font is available for purchase in the Shop on theydrawandcook.com.

*Also, be sure to visit *They Draw & Travel*, for travel maps created by artists from around the world.
theydrawandtravel.com

Made in the USA
Charleston, SC
01 May 2013